# WHEN THE TUNNELS MEET

# WHEN THE
# TUNNELS
# MEET

## CONTEMPORARY
## ROMANIAN POETRY

### EDITED BY
# JOHN FAIRLEIGH

## BLOODAXE BOOKS

Copyright © John Fairleigh 1996
Poems and translations © authors and translators
as listed on pages 7-10

ISBN: 1 85224 305 8

First published 1996 by
Bloodaxe Books Ltd,
P.O. Box 1SN,
Newcastle upon Tyne NE99 1SN.

Bloodaxe Books Ltd acknowledges
the financial assistance of Northern Arts.

Cover printing by J. Thomson Colour Printers Ltd, Glasgow.

Printed in Great Britain by
Cromwell Press Ltd, Broughton Gifford, Melksham, Wiltshire.

# CODA

Maybe we knew each other better
When the night was young and unrepeated
And the moon stood still over Jericho.

So much for the past; in the present
There are moments caught between heart-beats
When maybe we know each other better.

But what is that clinking in the darkness?
Maybe we shall know each other better
When the tunnels meet beneath the mountain.

LOUIS MACNEICE

# ACKNOWLEDGEMENTS

I would like to thank the following people who have contributed in many ways to the preparation of this anthology. In Romania, Gabriel Gafita of the Romanian Ministry of Foreign Affairs; Sînziana Dragos; Augustin Buzura, Carmen Firan and Vlad Pavlovici of the Romanian Cultural Foundation; Claus Henning, Aura Vlad and Eve Patten of the British Council; Mircea Martin and Denisa Comanescu of the Univers publishing house; Maria Berza; Maria Caramitru; Alexandra Cornilescu; Mima Griva; Andrei Marinescu; Andrei Plesu; Dani Popescu; Virginia Sorescu.

In Ireland, Peter Lyner of the British Council in Belfast; Brian Ferran and Ciaran Carson of the Arts Council of Northern Ireland; Edna Longley; Edward McCamley; Una McCarthy; Joan and Kate Newmann; Philip Orr; Michael Quinn; Gary Sloan; Damian Smyth; David Torrans; Brian Walker.

Laurence Cassidy of the Arts Council of Ireland; Micheal O'Siadhail and Marc Caball of the Ireland Literature Exchange; Peter Sirr of the Irish Writers' Centre; Theo Dorgan of *Poetry Ireland*.

Thanks are due to the Arts Council / An Chomhairle Ealaíon and to the Arts Council of Northern Ireland for providing grants to cover the cost of fees to the authors of the translations in this book.

The drawings of the poets are by Mircea Dumitrescu. The poem 'Coda' by Louis MacNeice is reprinted with the kind permission of David Higham Associates Ltd.

The versions in this book are based on literal translations by Simeon Dumitrache and Heather Brett. Special thanks are due to them for their work and for their commitment to the project.

JF

*for Ion Caramitru & Micaela Caracas*

# CONTENTS

# INTRODUCTION

The Romania that was one of the most tyrannical regimes in post-war Eastern Europe was no secret to observers of the old communist order. Even Ceaucescu could not stop news seeping through to the West of vicious repression of dissent, the destruction of much of the physical landscape of the countryside and the systematic demolition of historic architecture in the towns. The euphoria of Ceaucescu's fall in December 1989 was shared around the world, but it was not long before the name of Romania again was associated with unpalatable facts of life there – the plight of orphans and the handicapped, the struggle for democratic institutions and the fragility of an ill-managed economy.

Such facts about Romania are a part of the common knowledge of recent European history; but surviving in the common consciousness, independent of historical data, is another Romania – the Romania of the imagination. The names of the country and its province of Transylvania suggest dark forests in a place set apart from time; Bucharest, once recognised as the 'Paris of the East', evokes the image of an extravagant interwar café-society, emblematic of the privileged social elite of Central and Eastern Europe waywardly facing into its destruction. Such images of rural gothic and urban expressiveness have been the inspiration of compelling fictions such as Bram Stoker's *Dracula* and Olivia Manning's *Balkan Trilogy*, which in turn have amplified the mythology about the place.

It happens that Stoker and Manning have roots in Ireland, another country which despite an often tragic recent history is a place of escape for the romantic imagination. And just as the Irish may have shared and contributed to fanciful notions of Romania, it would seem that Romanians have picked up on many of the perhaps too flattering international perceptions of Ireland. During the 1970s and 80s when Ceaucescu imitated Mao in attempting to sever the cultural community from contaminating foreign influences, visions of Ireland were one opening to the forbidden world outside. This island on the far side of Europe offered an identity beyond the nightmarish present, in the sensing of a common racial inheritance through the Celts who had settled the lands around the Black Sea as early as the 3rd century BC; it affirmed a beleaguered religious belief in that it was Irish monks who were seen as having re-Christianised Europe in the 6th and 7th centuries, and the people of modern Ireland seemed to revere religion in their constitution

and national life; Ireland's rich tradition of literature and music
showed how small nations could conserve their spirit and identity
despite internal hardship and the threat of physical and cultural
invasion by large and predatory neighbours.

During the time between the communist takeover in 1947 and
the dramatic events of December 1989, and particularly during the
later Ceaucescu years, actual contacts between writers and the rest
of the non-communist world had to be tentative. Tourism into
Romania was encouraged as a source of Western currency but
socialising with local people was strictly discouraged. Some in-
coming academic and cultural visits, and occasional trips abroad by
Romanian artists and writers, were sanctioned so that Romanian
achievements might be recognised and savoured, but too many
links, even with vetted foreigners, could place an individual under
suspicion, threatening career and liberty. Despite these restrictions,
many poets and other creative artists dared to maintain inter-
national contacts. This meant that friends abroad could appreciate
the extent of their courage in challenging the repression and mis-
information of the state.

Among the collections of poetry drawn out from Romania dur-
ing these times was Bloodaxe's production in 1987 of *The Biggest
Egg in the World*, versions of Marin Sorescu by a group of poets
which included Seamus Heaney, Michael Longley and Paul Muldoon
(working from literal translations by Ioana Russell-Gebbett). This
book originated in Belfast which Sorescu had managed to visit on
rare approved journeys abroad and it was part of a developing
connection between poets in Ireland and Romania. After the revo-
lution of 1989, the previously tenacious but necessarily cautious
contacts were able to develop freely. Poets travelled between the
two countries to give readings, joint translation sessions were
arranged in writers' retreats in rural Ireland and Transylvania, and
translated poems began to appear frequently in Irish and Romanian
journals. Many of these literary connections over the years had
originated in chance meetings and friendships, but as they devel-
oped it became clear that there were deep affinities between the
poets in their themes, and striking parallels between the two
countries in the way poets were expected to articulate private
thoughts and public conscience.

Yeats during the struggle leading to Southern Irish independence
in 1921, and Heaney during the recent 25 years of violence in
Northern Ireland, could be looked to for inspiration, explanation
and solace. In Romania, during the repression of the Ceaucescu

years, poets like Sorescu played a somewhat similar role, drawing heavily on the history of the country, its struggles against invaders and its rich store of folk tales to help keep the individual and national spirit alive. Other poets were openly confrontational, risking more than has yet been expected of their Irish counterparts; Blandiana was banned a second time in the mid-1980s for stealthily getting into print a verse which included the lines 'I believe that we are a vegetal people...Who has ever seen/ a tree in revolt?', and Dinescu was placed under house arrest for daring to have published abroad an open challenge to the regime.

In the past few years, besides its appearances in literary magazines, contemporary Irish poetry has become further known in Romania through its necessary inclusion in academic courses of literature in the English language; Romanian poetry has been circulating in the West through the efforts of publishers such as Bloodaxe and Forest Books, and the generous commitment of Fleur Adcock, Michael Hamburger and other poets-turned-translators. However, in the new openness after the revolution there seemed to be a need for comprehensive and broadly based anthologies of Irish poets in Romanian and Romanian poets in English. Why not build on the existing tradition of friendship between the poets and ask them to work on two such volumes? In planning this project I consulted with publishers, readers and critics in Ireland and Romania, asking them to make a personal choice from the poets now writing in their own country. Out of the broad consensus which emerged, ten poets from each place were invited to participate in the preparation of the two anthologies: the Romanian and Irish were paired and each partner agreed to produce versions of the other's work. The Romanian poets in English were to be published by Bloodaxe; the Irish poets in Romanian by the Univers publishing house in Bucharest, an addition to its impressive list of previously banned or unobtainable world literature.

In the preparation of this volume, initial translations of the Romanian poems were made for the participating Irish poets by Romanian novelist Simeon Dumitrache and the young Irish poet Heather Brett: living in Ireland they were able to offer whatever further guidance or interpretation was needed as the work progressed. Some of the poets felt that the Dumitrache/Brett initial translations were distractingly good, too near a finished poem, so further and deliberately more literal translations were made for them by Stefania Hirtopanu, an English literature student from Bucharest University.

In seeking to recreate the Romanian texts, the Irish poets used a variety of approaches; in some poems they attempted a close following of the original lines, while in others they felt that a freer interpretation better represented the spirit of the original. An issue for the Irish poets, as for readers of their versions, is the extent to which one should delve back into the Romanian social and political context in the search for meanings. Many of the poems reflect aspects of the human spirit and condition that do not need to be fixed in a particular place or time, but others draw their power very directly from the circumstances in which they were written; the metaphors and the code of the messages from poet to reader cannot begin to be understood without a knowledge of the social and political world into which they were born.

The reality for artists in Ceaucescu's Romania was that while they had considerable social status, and access to influencing opinion, they were severly circumscribed in how they might use this privileged position. The regime was strongly supportive of the arts as an expression of national identity and pride, and as a means of reinforcing the brand of ideology it wanted Romanians to internalise and to present to the world outside. Even modest-sized provincial towns had their theatres, there were dozens of literary magazines, and many books were published in editions of hundreds of thousands. Much of this activity was of course hagiographic of the regime, some of it bland diversion; what it could never be was an open and honest expression of what the artist might want to say. The result was that artists, or other citizens of independent mind, had to speak in code, building a cover device or scrambler into every reaction or expression or opinion. During the particularly oppressive late 1980s, a distinguished actor and his wife were allowed to make a brief cultural trip to the United Kingdom and I met them in London before travelling on together to Belfast. A London shopkeeper, making welcoming conversation, asked us where we were going next. 'Dublin,' my Romanian friend interjected quickly. Later, when I asked him why he had said 'Dublin' when we were in fact going to Belfast, he explained 'Oh, it is best never to say anything too exactly.'

It was against this background of the necessity for obfuscation in the public expression of fact or feeling that the poets in this volume had to operate for all their working lives before 1989. But though they were monitored and in constant danger of being accused of they knew not what subversion, their readers expected from them strong signals of defiance of the regime and a confirmation that one was not mad in maintaining independent judgement: this was a society which falsified even the official register of temperatures to induce belief that winter was not so cold or summer not so hot. Poets were responsible, too, for the rallying of depressed spirits. Surrounded by the surveillance web of the Securitate and its agents, people were warily independent in their internal lives; thoughts that might not risk exploration even with good friends could be shared in a safe and private communion with the printed word of the poet. Such elements of Ceaucescu's bizarrely repressive society, and the role of the poet within it, have to be recognised in the reading of many of the Romanian poems. The special gift of the Irish poets to their partners in the versions prepared for this volume is that, while strongly aware of the context of the poems, they have recreated them not as mere disguised political tracts but as fresh and universal poems possessing the complexity and imagination that characterised the originals.

All but a few of the poems by which the Romanian poets chose to be represented in this anthology were written before the events of December 1989 which were to change, perhaps utterly for some, their role. During these days of turmoil which saw the downfall of Ceaucescu many of the poets, including Dinescu, turned to action on the streets:

> I thought poetry hid under the heron's wing
> or deep in the woods
> but like a prophet driven from the desert by oil rigs gurgling
> I'm ready to talk it out with reality.
>     I was wrong, wrong as can be.
> Just now, I'm smashing this wall with a pickaxe.
>     See

When the actor and popular leader Ion Caramitru, on his way to the television station to tell the nation that Ceaucescu had been deposed, failed to persuade Sorescu to join him in his tank, it was the younger Dinescu he asked to come with him to make the historic announcement. Who but a poet would be a credible voice from the past and the proper symbol of what should be the openness and integrity of the new order? In the first weeks after the events of December, many of the poets including Blandiana and Dinescu were active in the Salvation Front coalition, but soon they withdrew in protest at the resurfacing into government of too many of the old guard and their ways; both poets now are active in opposition, Blandiana as one of the leaders of the broadly based Civic Alliance and Dinescu as editior of a new satirical and anti-government magazine. In later elections Crasnaru became a member of the lower house of the new parliament and Doinas a senator. Sorescu in 1994-95 was Minister of Culture.

For the profession of poetry, this is an impressive record of public service, both as a lifeline to sanity in the grim years up to 1989 and as a source of leadership and guidance in the times of revolution and political change. But what is to be the continuing function of poets in Romania now that political participation is open, and information and opinions proliferate in the dozens of journals being sold on the streets? Should they be taking advantage of the new freedoms for which they fought so long, exercising their weight in the public debate and even joining in the party politics of the still fragile democratic system? For some of the poets this role as citizen may indeed take precedence over their poetry. The risk for them is that the traditional aura around poets as people of sensibility and superior insight might be diminished by the setbacks that may well befall poets in action, and that their authority thereafter will be lessened. Sorescu, characteristically modest and self-deprecating, said that in the weeks after the revolution people kept coming to ask for his advice, but that they did not come back because his advice so often was wrong. He did, nonetheless, accept the post of Minister of Culture and as a consequence suffered the loss, at least temporarily, of some of the enormous affection in which he had long been held.

For the poets choosing to speak only through their poetry, problems different to those of the old days emerge. No longer on offer are the generous subsidies to produce volumes of poetry in tens, even hundreds, of thousands. Nor is there likely to be such demand; in the open market of ideas and dissent there are many competitors. But the traditional role of the poet in Romanian society might yet be restored. The critic Ognyan Stamboliev wrote of Sorescu in the days before the revolution that his bond with his readers was that he 'mime-like, observes and comments on the modern world, on human relationships, and gropes for the dimensions of life and death, of fate and altruistic sacrifice'. As disillusion grows with the perceived failures of the new democratic government and with the inequalities and injustices that come with free enterprise and individual liberty, such reflections shared in private may again configure the relationship between the Romanian poets and the Romanian people.

JOHN FAIRLEIGH
*Institute of Irish Studies, Queen's University, Belfast*

# CEZAR BALTAG

## *versions by*
# DEREK MAHON

CEZAR BALTAG was born in 1939 in the Bukovina region. He belongs to what
is recognised in Romania as the very distinctive generation of poets of the
1960s; this was a period when the régime allowed a slight relaxation in the
demand that literature be only socialist and realist, and poets were able to
experiment with more abstract themes and structures. Since graduating in
philology from the University of Bucharest, Baltag has published many vol-
umes of poetry, essays and translations. He has also edited several impor-
tant literary magazines, and currently is Editor-in-Chief of *Romanian Life*.
His poetry reflects his interests in mythology and the history of religion.
His collection, *The Unicorn in the Mirror*, the title-poem of which is inc-
luded in this anthology, was published in 1975.

## On the threshold


A sentence in a dream: 'Don't go,
didn't you see the state of him? Don't go.'
Toward Cygnus like an apple
the sun falls;
and the candle wails
as if to escape the flame,
the bed, books, clothes, real life itself...
One day this century
an apple falls, and the scared dove
flies off from its cushion
with a scything sound.

Death, an actor in the dark, shouldering
the silence of a door,
comes on slowly, cries out in 'amazement',
raises a lamp, sheds light
and, all at once, you are whispering
like a bat lost in an endless tunnel.

An apple falls and the earth
clings tightly round its seeds.
Goodness is absolute, but the apple
is in love with the fall.

Once someone lived in you,
someone you didn't know
and whom you'll never forget;
someone is falling slowly and his bleak cry
is lost as if he were asleep.

The dove circling you
presages ice.

# Like the sun

How many meanings
can one translate
from the cry of a bird?

Yes?

No?

The middle term is missing
which neither affirms
nor denies
and without it
man
is a dead duck.

So make it up.

# The last stop

Station to station
hour to hour
kilometre to kilometre
tunnel to tunnel

until

the train on which I've come
enters the mirror

what mirror?

## A sign

I travel a hair-line
high
above a precipice

where once in a while
against my will
my gaze is drawn
downward.

        I'm up here
and an invisible
bird suddenly calls
I'm up here

A sign
my wings are not on fire
not yet

A sign
the sun is not dead
yet

## Thirst

The shadow
of a tree twists
on the wall.

A bird
stabs the leaves
like a quick knife.

The wind blows
and the tree stoops
to drink its own shadow.

# Dialogue in stone

A peal of thunder
still echoes ominously
in my deaf ear;

the sky reeled
from arc to arc
in a flash of lightning

as if, down here,
I slept under a bell
you have been ringing without pause,
an intolerable noise –

as if all hearing froze
between us while you beat
at my stone ear-drums with your fists,
there's no one to tell you what happened
and daylight comes again
at an insomniac pace.

It's no good, I can't hear you;
all sound refuses me.

# Echo in the seed

Still deeper
in the heart of the forest,
deeper still...

When I no longer hear
the child
who calls me
I shall know then for sure
I have lost my way –

till when
I do not want
to see the moss on the trees.

Till when keep
calling me, keep calling
me, keep...


## The cry


Too late your oars
have closed the water
into the curious ovals
that sustain the world.

Does there exist a visible bridge,
a path of beams taking their light
from nowhere, towards your heart
silent now like an anvil
when the pounding has ceased?

Its heart stone is as far
from us as the sun
and weighed down by a shadowy paradox.


## The interior umbrella


Divine caul
of a dark child
as yet unborn

parachute of despair

when I opened it
it rained stars
and invisible children

## The unicorn in the mirror

The galloping white...
the white horse galloping
among sharp rocks and thorn-bushes...
Prepare a magic bridle, a crown of blood
for a white lily
the hunt pursues in vain;
a bridle of blood for the white horse
galloping down a road of virgin snow
between two wintry rivers.

A bridle of blood for the white horse galloping...

'The unicorn can only be caught
with a mirror, a pure desire
sweetening the impossible;
its object is a reflection.'

A maiden sleeps on the water; white horse.
Death is a bed of running water,
death is the direction. Don't wake her.
Death sleeps on the river holding a mirror.

A river that mirrors cannot be named,
a river named can never mirror:
the maiden too is nameless, names are hunters.
The unicorn looks to left and right: which way?

I am a field snowed under, galloping,
a white field running across a white field.
Hunters are running inside my ear;
water, save me from this chase,
albeit I came to the fire that I might burn.

Snow, your name be glorified!

Cloth spun to left and right,
there is no water, only flame,
flame-water mirroring flame,
a cloth of flame spinning flame,
a white lily galloping towards flame.

Before opening his eyes he sees
the Mirror running to meet its Son
or only to listen, perhaps, to its heart in the tree:
the maiden Daphne giving birth to the tree,
Daphne enclosed in her own child.

A lily of flame galloping in the mirror
escapes and is caught,
escapes once more and is caught;
a mirror is the gate
where a white horse confronts a white horse.

'The unicorn can only be caught
with a mirror, a pure desire
sweetening the impossible.'

The flame holds a wooden mirror,
he comes to inspect his face;
the world-horse dies in the wooden womb
as Daphne ignites the tree and so gives birth.

The ears are on fire, *nivalis dei*, the eyes on fire,
the tongue on fire the day it flows,
the heart of fire drives blood of fire
through arteries of fire,
the sound of fire strikes the ear-drum of fire.

Snow, show me your mirror.
A little to the left and I disappear,
a little to the right and you see me again.
I'm joining the fire and the whole fire is mine.

White horse, white horse, white horse
known to all by its signs and to nobody by nothing,
snow-fire fed on snow-fire,
a maiden burning in its ear
while in her mirror once more there gallops a white horse.

*Quod inferius est sicut quod superius*

A mirror is the gate
where a white horse confronts a white horse.

# ANA BLANDIANA

*versions by*
## SEAMUS HEANEY

ANA BLANDIANA was born in 1942 in Transylvania. She is the daughter of
an orthodox priest and her work displays strong roots in her religious up-
bringing and in the folk poetry and fairy-tales of Transylvania. While still
at school her writing was published in literary magazines and anthologies.
After graduating from the University of Cluj, she worked as an editor and
columnist with several literary journals. In the years before 1989 she re-
ceived many honours from the Writers' Union and the Romanian Academy,
but she was also on several occasions banned because of open challenges
to the régime. She was awarded the International Herder Prize for Litera-
ture in 1982. Currently she is President of the Romanian Pen Club. Active
in the revolution of 1989, she was briefly involved in the Salvation Front
in the days before it became a political party. She was one of the founders,
and is now the leader, of the opposition Civic Alliance movement. Her work
is available in Britain in *The Hour of Sand: Selected Poems 1969-1989*,
translated by Peter Jay and Anca Cristofovici (Anvil Press, 1989).

## Do you remember the beach

Do you remember the beach
Covered with splintered glass,
That beach
Where we couldn't walk barefoot?
And the way you would gaze
At the sea, and gaze, all absorbed, and say
You were listening to me?
Do you remember
The gulls going wild, wheeling
Round and round as the bells
Chimed out behind us somewhere
In churches that had
Fish for their patron saints?
And how you headed away
At a run
Towards the surf, yelling back
That you needed distance
To be able to see me.
Then the gulls,
The swirl of the snow,
The spray, all of them mingled,
And I would look on
With a kind of desperate elation
As your feet marked the sea,
The sea that would close like an eyelid then
Where I waited and looked.

# The country we come from

Let's talk about
The country we come from.
I am from summer,
A homeland so frail
The fall of a leaf
Could crush it to nothing.
Still, the sky there is gravid with stars
And sags so near to the earth, sometimes
Before you know where you are it is all
Brushed air, grass-tickle, star-giggles
And flowers: so many flowers
Ablaze like so many suns
Hurting your eyes,
Drying them up in their sockets.
And meanwhile round suns are hanging
From every tree.
Where I come from
The only thing missing is death.
There happiness is so abounding,
You keep drifting off, you are sleepy,
So sleepy, so sleepy.

# Sometimes I dream

Sometimes I dream of my body
Caught in a trawl-net of wrinkles
And pulled like a dead weight through snow;
This happens on a hard-frozen, dazzling beach
Beside a clear bay.
I never see the fisherman
But I know he's your father:
What I do see each time
Is the wrinkle-net and my body
Like a catch in its meshes, hauled up
Into the pure, unknowable dream
Of the morning I die,

So peaceful
You do not enter it,
So silent I do not call out:

Everything is sleeping open-eyed
And the one thing that moves –
A light within that light, an echo –
Is a whisper-weak curse
That frays and unravels the net
So that I slip out again
To the timeless, immaculate waters.

## Maybe there's somebody dreaming me

Maybe there's somebody dreaming me
And that's why my gestures have turned
So slack and soft-edged,
Their purpose forgotten half-way,
My every move idiotic,
Backsliding and groggy.
It explains these states of collapse
When my profile keeps fading
And all that I do melts away...
And whoever is dreaming me, maybe
Every now and again
He comes to his senses, dragged
Forcibly up from his sleep
And into his life,
The one that is real.
Which is why the shadows unnerve me
And I'm sometimes left hanging
On a melting thread of wet snow,
Not knowing if ever
He'll be able to get back to dreaming
So that something in my own life
Can happen to me.

# It's snowing hostility

It's snowing hostility.
There's hate in this snow coming down
On waters deep-frozen with hate,
On orchards that bloom for sheer badness,
On the embittered, suffering birds.
It's snowing as if the snow meant
To smother the life of this people
Aswim in their gifts.
It's snowing with a ferocity
That's only too human,
It's snowing with venom.
And is no one surprised?
Is there nobody else who remembers
That in the beginning this snow
Was a snowfall of love?
Now it is late
And the terrible blizzard's still blowing
And there's nothing for it, I think,
But to wait
And be there
For the famishing wolves,
At their disposal.

# The morning after I die

The morning after I die
Will be cool, like those misty September dawns
When the dog-days are over
And I blink awake in white air, making strange
At a woolly light in the trees.
And because it's September, I'll have come to
Very early and – again like September –
Be lonely enough to keep hearing
The air drip-dripping towards noon
Down the wet cheeks of quinces;

I'll be in a drowse,
Praying to get back to sleep
For a little while longer,
Lying there, never moving,
Eyes closed, my face in the pillow,
As the deafening silence beats louder
And louder and wakens me up more and more.

The start
Of that eternal day
Will be like a morning in autumn.

## Inhabited by a song

The song isn't mine,
It just passes through me sometimes,
Uncomprehended, untamed,
Lightly dressed in my name;
The way the gods in the old days
Would pass among people
Dressed in a cloud.

I don't know when it will come,
I don't know when it will go
Or where it is all the while
It isn't inside me:
My whole destiny is to attend
On the whim of a marvellous thing.

Inhabited by a song,
Forsaken by a song,
Maybe even the widow of a song
(My unknown beloved)
I am not the one for your laurels –
Except insofar as I've been
Its servant, humble and faithful
Right to the end.

## Loneliness

Loneliness is a town
Where everyone else is dead.
The streets are clean,
The street-markets empty,
Suddenly everything's in a true light
Through being deserted – exactly
The way it was meant to be.
Loneliness is a city
Where it's always snowing
Prodigiously, and no footsteps ever
Profane the layered
Drift of the light.
And you alone, the unsleeping eye
Keeping an eye on the sleepers, you
See, comprehend, and can't have enough
Of a silence so pristine
Nobody fights there,
Nobody's lied to,
And even the tear in the eye
Of the abandoned animal
Is too pure to hurt.
On the border
Between suffering and death,
Loneliness is a happy town.

## Hunt

I never have been in pursuit of words.
All I ever looked for
Was traces of their passage
Like the long silver haul
Of sunlight sweeping the grass
Or moonblinds drawn on the sea.

The shadows of words
Are what I hunted –
And hunting these is a skill
Best learned from the elders.
The elders know
That nothing is more precious
In a word
Than the shadow it casts
And words with no shadow to cast
Have lost their word-souls.


## As if


As if the light itself
Were merely a plant, as if the stars
Sent down their thin rays
Like capillary roots
Sucking at me, to extract
Their mysterious nutrient.
Astral blooms flock to the scalpel
Like crows to the plough.

The size of this field of light scares me.
With so many flowers to feed, I'm worn
To the bone, fulfilled and woozy with love.
And whom can I call for assistance?
Will nobody rid me, root, stem and branch,
Of this star-sprouting garden,
Burst the galactic, numinous dykes
And make way for the ocean of darkness?

# MIRCEA CĂRTĂRESCU

## *versions by*
## MEDBH McGUCKIAN

MIRCEA CĂRTĂRESCU, born in Bucharest in 1956, is regarded in Romania as one of the most original voices of the younger generation, breaking from the earlier tradition of romantic lyricism and allusion to record very directly the experiences of youth and the city. After graduating from the University of Bucharest, he taught for a few years at a secondary school before working for the Writers' Union and becoming editor of *Critical Notes*. He is currently a lecturer in Romanian language and literature at the University of Bucharest. His extensive range of published work includes, besides eight books of poetry, collections of prose, essays and literary criticism.

## To an artiste

Playfellow, my pillow has slept with your head
while I smoke on. We kept each other
awake for long enough, the vodka bottle
is half-naked at its thickest part:
your cigarettes are down to a guess of two.

Our up-times or whatever sex we mimed
between teasing debates and French library
films, are packed up with the season's luggage.
You will transfer your art to others,
I will make it with different rhymes.

But sleep your fill on my pillow, guest:
I can't idealise your boy's chest
into Baudelaire's mulatto – haven't a clue
what to do with tomorrow at the station:
we'll both drag our bags around the flagged
platform, post square envelopes till summer...

You shine already absent, minus your glasses.
How worth seeing, the heavy moon through pane 21!
But our days and nights of "love" are wrapped up
with the season. You will teach others your magic,
I will learn it over in my rhymes...

## Slightly in mourning

Pay me love for love,
owe me and be owned.
There's a fair sun, the sky
is sky-blue, with blue clouds:
Life ought to be fun!

Till the silver-plated cord frays
and the gilt goblet is in smithereens...

The lowlands are green, the mainroads dusty,
the highlands golden, the viaducts breathe brick:
you're a girl-child that has weathered your virtue
all through the vacation – your mother's poor but honest.

Can't you be generous, stop tantalising,
taking your bad moods out on me?
Don't hold out for the wedding, take things easy,
when you caress, do it without thinking.

I've had it with 'passionate affairs' – I daresay
you've had your fill of them too,
gnawing your pillow, endless tennis
to drown the telephone quivering
like a point in a socket –
those scenes are a write-off.

Even though we're in the red,
let's take out a mortgage on life:
the silverplated cord frays
and the gilt goblet is in smithereens!

## Three Brothers Vodka

There was this friend of mine,
who thought nothing of squeezing his biro
into the eye of a cock-sparrow,
or knocking a nail into a dozing cat.

Once from the flat roof of a hospital
he hurled a white-coated bed-panel
down on to a passing engine-hood.

With schoolgirls, he was ruthless and depraved,
his favourite pastime was to bind victims
to doorhandles with countless reef-knots.

There were nights he howled in sleep,
imagining his utter loneliness in vast open deserts.
A conversation with him was like peeling
a mildewed lemon or your hand sinking
into a pile of spiders' webs.

As a youngster he was a nasty good-for-nothing,
but as he grew, you felt pity instead,
he was so nervous, awkward and hopeless
with women, could never look you straight
in the eye. A miserable dog,
God knows why a man like that
should experience life.

I'm on the top floor of the Three Brothers bar,
wondering about all this. It's packed,
the human race has not yet emerged
from prehistory, nor looks as if it will.
I sip my vodka, head reeling
from the nine-to-five day.
Two hours daily commuting in which
less and less, I read.

I get the bill for my black mood,
I'm almost, imagine, thirty;
going through the plate door, a sleety blast
pins me against the glass:
I'll be wet through
by the time I hit the sack.

## I'm smiling

It's not until some overweight shoppers
give me a dirty look
that I realise I'm smiling.
Smiling in the 109 bus, travelling
to work, it goes without saying
that a long drink of water
hanging out of a window
and smiling, doesn't cut much ice.
Nevertheless, the thought of you
brought on the perfunctory smile
like Pavlov's dog.

This morning I woke bathed
in ghastly nightmares of being
flayed alive, needles stabbing
my teeth like teaching a grammar lesson.
The odour of underclothes and petrol
permeates the bus, blocks of flats
are all that the window offers.

I smiled, I must have
kept smiling for some time.
I recalled how we crashed the theatre,
you in your shapeless saffron T-shirt,
myself in one that could have done
with a wash. The vestibule
sported couples dressed to the nines.
We were like something out of *Woodstock*.

At school the principal laid into me,
the secretary looked daggers.
The dried-out pot-plant had only a quarter
of its leaves. Trying to control my class,
I found the smile creeping back
so irresistibly, I had to face the blackboard.

## When love's what you need

When you need love there's none,
when you are mad for it, it's not returned.
When you are alone you are alone,
when you are down, there's no way you can explain.

When you feel like putting your arms around
someone, there's no one. When you feel
like a phone-call no one's in.
When you're in the pits, who gives a damn?

Stay with me, think about me,
be good to me, don't drive me crazy with jealousy,
don't leave, another break-up would finish me,
stay with me, take my part.

Understand me, I don't want a wild life,
or even conversation, be my live-in partner,
let's drop the golden rule, that sex's a jungle,
let's compromise, let's get engaged...!

But I'm out of line, love's not on the menu.
When you need it or are mad for it,
it's never returned. When you're in the pits,
no woman wants to know.

## Adriana

About six o'clock, at the news stand,
in the sultry dusk of an exhausted September,
you could still get away with a thin sweater.
I caught a glimpse of myself in a petrol-coloured
windscreen, I was looking a million dollars,
I felt on top of the world.
I had to ask the ice-cream vendor twice
what time it was, before my date
suddenly appeared. I grabbed her hand.
It was nice out, as I was telling you,
she was wearing peppermint jeans,
no make-up apart from a mauve dot
on each eyelid. I was not in love,
but she offered me the illusion
that I had a girlfriend, that someone
gave *that* about me, and at least
I was holding quite a good-looking
chick by the hand.
We walked over chatting
to the 23rd of August Stadium,
to the parachute training tower.
But what more can I say,
than that we sat in the curved
back seats of the deserted rink
under the metallic
panning of the searchlights,
and it was fine?
There might have been a vague
smell of sulphur off her, but
she had sprayed her hair with Magie
Noire, old for so young a girl.
When darkness fell, we moved off,
under the electronic scoreboard,
tracked by midges.
I meant to explain
that in fact she wasn't in love
with me either, and had never
been in love in her life;

but it felt all right,
and we actually spent
some not entirely unhappy evenings together.


## The blonde beast


What a blonde beast, pausing at the jeweller's window!
A creature like you simply oughtn't
to be allowed to circulate at your own free will.
Christ, what nipples through your fox-coloured
Coca-cola T-shirt! What an animal lurks
behind the lattice of your blue jeans,
under the padlock of your zip.
What raw meat joints you must be devouring,
purring like a lioness,
you ultra female you.

Not the ordinary fare of mortals –
not to die from the strychnine of your hair
one would need Citroën sheet-iron armour,
banknote bandages.
Now you gaze at yourself among the ladies' watches
that turn your face into a galaxy –
you're the sort that prefers quartz.
Men scarcely dressed as men
and two decorators in paint-starred
overalls, caps down over their eyes,
are dazzled by you.

Autumn tempts me to compare
your back to the harvest moon,
in my insignificance.
If I won a Nobel prize it would be
the money that would impress you.
There's no way I can be seen on TV
or be a native of Lebanon.

Blonde beast, you glide to the next window,
Casio's for eleven, thirteen thousand.
You have a fine muzzle, cruelly rouged,
your teeth gleam, your eyes are sharp
or foolish, who cares?
You exist in a sprayed, shampooed, aesthetic
labyrinth of fashion and hairy hands.
I harvest from bending over
my typewriter mere disgust.
One of your breasts alone
is worth more than my collected works,
as you drift through the leaves
on the spoor of the Dunhill in your handbag.

## Do you know a countryside where
## the lemon trees are in bloom?

I am waiting at *State Circus* stop for streetcar 26.
The whole street is gold-lit, the saplings have such a wealth
of leaves, not even a Renaissance artist could capture them on canvas.
I lust after blue-jeaned broads in out-sized T-shirts –
JOGGING is spelt across one's flat chest – I stop, turn,
a number 5 draws up and as I finger
its burning crimson a line occurs to me,
I even get the words:
'This summer we've all became car-mechanics,
we all tinker with pieces of the clouds' undercarriage...'

May's half-spent, I am suffering from sunstroke,
children present their teachers
with rough lilac boughs and cellophaned
lily-of-the-valley. Direct sun-gazing
leaves a splinter in your eye,
a mauve slipper, faces and hatbands
of violet light. Bottled sun,
hairshirt moon, this summer
we've all become a manner
of car mechanic, we all tinker
with pieces of the clouds' undercarriage,
we all unscrew the axle of the flowers.

Finally, after a string of 24s and 4s,
a 26 arrives – I shove aboard and bag a spot
near the rear window.
The brilliance of the street is suffocating
but your heart is closed to it, being without love.
The shop-windows no longer mean anything to you.
You can write nothing but dull and worthless epistles.
I open Himmelmann's *Utopian Past*
with its handsome azure dustjacket,
and read Goethe's view on statues.
Bucharest, to right and to left, is and is not.

# A day-and-a-half for the banana-fish

A day-and-a-half for the banana-fish:
I catch a 90 and ride as far as the university.
Who would credit, beloved reader, it's mid-December?
The electric clock/thermometer was showing 15 degrees,
the pekes had abandoned their pied waistcoats.
The twigs on the bushes seemed to be trying
to turn a little green,
and the architectural institute
was dissolving its ancient limestone
sunbeams everywhere, rose-orange windows
packed with skirts, shirts and sweaters,
deodorants and shaving-cream.
And in front of the café, incredible sight,
ten crates of Pepsi for sale on the open street.

What a day! A day-and-a-half for the banana-fish!
Herds of fox-skinned women under a summer sky.
I took two bottles of effervescent Pepsi
and sat at a white cast-iron table
on the sun-laquered terrace,
my eyes straining in the light.
I had left my sheepskin jerkin at home
but my synthetic jacket started to smell
of body-heat. Two students opposite
were drinking Pepsi too, one a dove-eyed
beauty with my favourite kind of hair,
dark streaked with gold highlights,
not too curly. Her fur coat hung open
and her shape was defined through
an air-coloured blouse. Beloved reader,
the world colours were so in flux
I was scared to breathe, in case I'd absorb
some passer-by or vehicle or the university
would engulf me. The girls left,
but I soon found a replacement,
and when I finished my Pepsi
I dived into the confusion of the traffic
then caught the trolley back home.
A morning-and-a-half for the banana-fish!

## My everyday dream

I'm not sure if it's only fin-de-siècle accidie,
autumn maddening us all, laundering away
our jaundiced bowers and the blood from the mill-bricks,
wafting the unwashed savour of deprivation
and abandoned railways – is it something else?
I'm not sure, but it's obvious
that the whole world, on footpaths,
in factories and cake-shops,
at draughty bus-stops,
men, their spouses, teenagers,
girls in kneesocks and gymslips,
with oversized earrings,
repudiate the vast social organism
of families and babies in carriers,
even their flesh and blood, veins and nerves,
to imagine under the lightbulbs
what happiness must be:
happiness at school, at the office,
at table, in the fields, in bed.
And Boots overflows
with every kind of character
queuing up at the counter
half-out-of-their-minds, for happiness
in the form of ointments or diazepam.

To be honest, this is how I feel
a lot of the time myself.
Particularly when, after about three hours'
teaching at number 41, I go to eat
at auto-mechanic, on the first floor,
in the fragrance of overalls and meat-jelly,
in the gossip of cash and spark-plugs.
I sit with my meatballs and a glass
of raspberry juice, but I'm not really eating
because I'm in the middle of this dream.
My dream of happiness is a kind of asylum
or small hostel, buried in a leaf-bearing forest,
a building with snowy walls and inside it
a warmed dormitory, with a dozen

or at most fifteen beds, perfumed with fresh sheets,
in other words, an infirmary, but minus
injections and medicines.
a sanatorium without hypodermics,
even a madhouse, without lobotomies or electric shocks.

There we would sit, a handful of pyjamaed creatures,
gaudy as possible, with lime and raspberry spots,
elephants, Donald Ducks, giraffes,
tying with cords, like files.
We'd stay put forever, curled under blankets,
chatting, twisting Rubikcubes, at mealtimes
being served grapefruit.
All alone, without papers or kinsmen,
with no decisions to make, we'd slumber
and saunter, gaze out of the window,
sit in the dusk with our souls on the heaters
reading fiction and American short-stories
by up-and-coming authors, a maze of plots
you can never wake from.
Without women – almost without men –
we'd grow old there, in total isolation,
in the purr of the boiler, in the gurgle
of the cistern, in the stir of the bedlinen,
listening to it beginning to snow
over the forest.
There would also be a table
at which I would write
everything that goes on in my mind,
I'd scribble lines and stories,
and keep a journal
with a neighbour beside me
soldering circuits
with a welding-iron,
by the light of an arc-lamp.
That's about the height of my desires,
if we're talking about happiness,
the same thing day after day,
the flavour of tin and grapefruit skin,
and lads with casual nicknames,
Fats, Rats, Bangers, ill-at-ease
in their motley pyjamas,

reading and studying
the snow-window.
Never to have to make a decision,
no one's well-being ever depending on you;
oh tender, white and loving cage,
in which to live free!

For the time being, I polish off my meatballs
and down the raspberry, then return
to stroll along a street
crammed with car bodies and motor machinery
and worn tyres. Yes –
everybody has their happiness.
And this is mine –
a snug bedroom
in a snowed-up forest.

# DENISA COMĂNESCU

## *versions by*
## EILÉAN NÍ CHUILLEANÁIN

DENISA COMĂNESCU was born in 1954 in Buzau. After graduating in Rom-
anian and English from the University of Bucharest, she joined the Univers
publishing house where she now is Editor-in-Chief. For her first volume of
poetry, published in 1979, she received the Debut Prize of the Writers'
Union. She has translated many English language poets into Romanian,
and selections from her own work were included in the two Forest Books
anthologies, *Silent Voices* (1986), and *Young Poets of a New Romania* (1991).
She is secretary of the Romanian Pen Club.

## Persephone

*'Here let thy clemency, Persephone...'*
EZRA POUND


Light flowed out from her body
as from the flowering linden
on the frozen soil –
tracing a grid
fantastic leafy forms
a stronger sun
would hold
a quiet sun –
and I had come
under that law.

Like ash-grey stones
only the sea
had ever handled
it looked to me like
pain.
fear
hatred.
I followed her I never trembled
I shared her light,
it was a holy place

where the blasphemers
embraced all of a sudden
faith.

Again the time drew close
for your return,
tender leech,
as if the old eyelid
were to slide up from an eye
transparent with memory.

Persephone,
my sister,
where is your clemency?

## An unforgiving joy

An image old still clear
transforms itself into a grain of sand
red-hot and luminous
thousands of glow-worms set off
through the blood
their small lamps shine out
through the snailshell of the ear
the sun drinks the salty drops
the echo wakens the birds bored stiff
in soft burrows.
I eat tinned food with a seashell
the sand
polishes the roof of my mouth
until it's as bright
as a skating-rink
waiting for the touch
of the singular skater.
One instant
the phosphorescent wave
rises high in the body.
All the breast
an unforgiving joy.

Up there
the steep wall
brick-red
in us
beating
like a heart
the sea.

## The world of language

Towards you there comes an apparition
and you create it out of words
but the darkroom of the brain
remains mysterious
like the trifling demons in a hermit's life.
Sometimes destroyer fantasies
dart through syllables
like the moth making its nest
in the soldier's purple wound.

The war is real.
Quiet nights and the moon
treacherous pauses
to give the nod for murder.
Words are shrinking.
The most fragile
the most solitary in all the world of language
I tried to save today.

Through the slashed vein of love
the morse notes
drip slowly:
*I will succeed. Later.*


## Hibernation

I need a line
give me one.
*The hint of fire in the lucerne.*
I would invent a godhead
but my mind is barren.
The spirit no longer fills up
a waste.
Bad steward! Who gave you this life in trust?
With pebbles and stones.
The earth swallows tracks of fire.
Give me a line.

## Fever in June

in up to my neck
decapitated
put a dockleaf on it
the beautician with the leg-wax told me,
no need for surgery
it'll heal itself
you'll grow a new head
*good as ever, strong and fine**
the ground went from under my feet
I left it far behind me
why did it go, the echo calls,
is that someone there at all?
no, my voice replies
as if I'd switched on a tape,
that someone isn't there at all
it's the sea, the doll that once called me mother
hand shivering in spasm like a foetus in the morning sink

it is my youth

* A quotation from a Romanian children's song,
not unlike 'London Bridge is falling down'.


## Breathing space

my right hand is a tube
and my right eye
and my mouth, a rusty tube in the morning
when I try to clean it with two fingers
the poison-grass buds in it
last summer in the sea your ankle was a hot pipe
with what desperation I caressed the smooth shinbone
a navel cord connecting me to the world, your ankle
a magnetic tube holding me still in life
and even still I pass through deep places like a wave left behind
and even still it is only through this that I breathe.

## Late call

pages filled, life torn apart
at a sheepfold in Bucovina
a man with bluish glasses softly goes away
gigantic dogs wrap their tongues around my hand
the steep side of the hill is like a sledge
and a tar-black stream in the valley calls for me
there in lukewarm water I am going to fall asleep
I have a cheque in my purse for the most demanding ferryman
what good mothers the dark waves

## Gaming machines

in a forest in Dorna children were collecting buds of pine
as they cheerfully firmly crushed all the branches that will never
        come again
I was dying for an embrace
one time a man had invented love for me
in a forest clearing, I was dying like then, I would say,
but otherwise, with that longing that means infinite distances
I recalled his rough hands, his thumb
scarred by a saw, the fragrance of his healthy skin
violently alongside the children I began
breaking the branches that will never come again

# The dragons of humiliation

A telephone rings in my mind
the way a mandrake pulled up by the roots
might cry.
All the taps are on
the living stream is drowning me.
Playful fish
in a shining river
about to leap into my lap.
Clear notes invite the heart
huddled in a boat
leaks never caulked
guts torn apart –
would pull me
towards the harmony
that wants me still.
O, fire and stake of humiliation
your dragons have eaten me up already.
A telephone rings in my mind
just as a mandrake pulled up by the roots
would cry.

## A smile in an endless sleep

A man asleep on a bench in front of the sanatorium –
as if for manna from heaven he has waited for those he loves
white and huddled –
from here in the valley he seems
a lamb biting at the green wood
I could get closer, could call him,
shake him awake, embrace him
but he has wiped out everybody from space and time
first thing he wiped out himself
like a leg eaten with gangrene
between two drops of *Neuleptil*
no human quivering,
if they arrived now, all those he loves,
sat in a circle as at an initiation
they would only find his smile in an endless sleep,
the yellow smile, the flower of the green wood.

# DANIELA CRĂSNARU

*versions by*
## THOMAS McCARTHY

DANIELA CRĂSNARU was born in 1950 in Craiova and graduated from the
university there in 1973. She made her literary debut in 1967, and there-
after published several volumes of poetry while working with different pub-
lishing houses. She has written many lyrics for children; children's litera-
ture is one of her specialities in her current role as Director of the Ion
Creanga publishing house. Fleur Adcock translated a collection of her
poetry, *Letters From Darkness*, published by Oxford University Press in
1991. Since the revolution Daniela Crasnaru has been active in politics and
has sat as a member of the lower house of the Romanian parliament.

## Lions of Babylon

This is one morning
in five thousand years.
Behold the lions of Babylon

in an underground chamber of the palace,
to the left and right of the scribe.
He it was
who never saw the sun,
who never saw the river,
nor the sea.
Leaning over his tablet of clay,
he describes the heavens
and makes a detailed picture
of a mighty river flowing
into the sea.

Nor has the slave with his story
ever seen the river
or the sun, or the sea.
He has heard this witness from another
who pressed his flesh to the clay
until he lost himself:
losing his blood,
losing his body to the outer light;
to the secret river when it enters the sea.

# Days of 1988
*(Fame)*


In vain you scribble poems!

'To be a famous European poet,' I was told
by a friend, 'you must be a cannibal.'
Not long ago darkness, hunger, cold
were common, inoffensive crumbs
from the communal word-hoard.
Just now it is a winter evening of '88,
the family at dinner, winter gaslight.

On a child's plate, a last piece of meat.
Hunger of conversation, tears in my throat:
tonight all the leftovers are mine;
she may not wipe her plate this time.
With frozen hands we spread the jam,
without speaking, without a look.
The simple bread of yesterday, or tomorrow.

Or tomorrow? A basic adverb of time.
Time is money? asks the child.
No, not for us. Time is fear.
With an atavistic drive, I look
at a child's leftovers:
my morsel today, and my humiliation.

I look at my mother's thin hands,
at the frail body of my own child.
'You have to be a cannibal, at least,
to be famous in Europe today.'
Not far off the point, to be sure.
In bloody regalia fame knocks at the door:
Europe will greet the spectre
it can hardly have waited for.

# My own private Hyde Park

By day I write obedient poems, peaceful and publishable.
But at night, with the blanket pulled over me,
looking inward, I journey illegally to Hyde Park,
a private Hyde Park within my exhausted heart.
And there I address an audience without reserve,
of deaf mutes. See their frenetic approval.
Towards dawn an angel appears, my guardian angel,
with a belt, a pistol and a multitude of stars.
'Hey, the fun's over. Who'd you think you are?'
he says.'Uttering your pathetic names:
Romania is nothing in the geopolitical game.
Land of little consequence, mere dusty tack-room
of the major powers. A bagatelle.
Stand down at once, get in the queue for milk.'

Dawn smashes the windows with its bloody sickle.

Ah yes! I shall write obedient poems.
I shall publish all my metaphors of avoidance.
But allow me to dry my pillow with an iron,
salty stains, shorthand notes from my private soapbox.
With this iron I shall erase the hot surface of night,
like a burgler who scrubs incriminating prints.
Today, as yesterday, I shall seek out
those bland synonyms for Cowardice, and for Terror.

## The poetry of camouflage

I have learned to be politic, efficient, well-behaved.
I have learned to wait and to stop waiting.
I have learned to regard words as loose, like ants
free within the parameters of my paper, building abstract edifices,

not knowing a thing about crises of the region
or the world, or affairs of the heart; those fashionable
opiates. So I have learned the word courage:
courage to be silent, as I was told, or not to be silent,

each more important. Whatever. I was told to choose.
I have learned not to choose anymore. That is why
I swallow sentences as stoically as a young child,
as in my childhood I swallowed cod-liver oil. 'Don't cry.

Now then, this will help you grow. You will feel sick
for a moment. Then it's over. It does you good.'
I'd like to believe my mother was right. That trick
with cod-liver oil has been replaced, as I replace words

right now, synonyms. I build circumlocutions.
Together with other poems, announcements, ads, whatever
can be found at the given moment on the page,
my poem is found among them, almost indistinguishable.
        The hunter

wearing camouflage is just like that, the safari truck,
the lizard on a stone. All lost in their landscape.
I should be pleased. My mother's voice, protective, tender:
'For a minute you'll feel sick. But it's good, you'll see. Don't cry.'

## Orpheus in the Underworld

I walk the streets of Frankfurt with a poet-friend.
He's been exiled from Romania these two years.
Lights illuminate us, advertise their new wares.
I smell vanilla ice-cream at one street-end.
We examine freedom's superficial face.
'It's great here,' he says. 'There's so much food.
But the poems won't come like at the old address.
I wrote my best work in the depth of unhappiness.
Here I can scream at authority, say anything loud,

but the substance of poetry is our familiar pain.
The more unhappy you are, the better you write.'
I stroll beside him in silence now,
trying to feel this freedom, but all in vain.
Can his theory be true? By God, if he's right
then we'll all be (shortly), genius-Romanians.

## A private affair

And where should I go?
My friend Gerhardt has relatives in Germany –
God willing, he will go there and be spared.
Eve, my friend, is Hungarian.
God willing, she too will rejoin her family.
In Hungary the prison bars are farther apart...

And me? Where could I go
when my native boundary is the Romanian tongue?
What became of Tarkovsky and Solzhenitsyn?
The West gets bored so quickly
of us Third World dissidents.
How funny we become, what a show!
One month, one year. We are exiled
from the front page to back-page news,
then to the common grave of gossip.

Ladies and Gentlemen!
Reader, these tears are tears indeed.
This life of mine is not an illusion;
this blood isn't an actor's paint.
No hard currency can pay for this,
although everything is business –
Love, friendship, liberty, belief, the arts:
everything can be bought and sold.

Yet we have one powerful advantage.
Here with us Death is still a private Art.
I exercise daily to be fit for my part.

## Writing lesson

That year, again, I rescue.

Our teacher speaks:
describe this brilliant cascade of water,
glorious in the sunshine.
I stare at the anaemic fibre
                    of water
trickling through the gutter's structure

and, humiliated, speak:
*I can't*, again *I can't*.
'You've no wings,' he complains,
'no fabric of metaphysics.
Repeat after me, white, brilliance, crystal, joy.'

Ah, white, brilliance, the word-corsets

of clean starched lace
through which, alas, reality bursts
with much impertinence,
like blood through a sterile dressing.
On the beach last year
I found the ultimate response –
a drowned man pulled ashore,

a brilliant cascade of water
rushing from his lungs.
I learned this with my eyes:
no immaculate petals,
no joy of butterfly wings.
Water and blood coagulate in sand.

'You will fail this year,'
the teacher says,
and pours me into space
from the school's seventh ledge.
He pretends not to notice.

I pretend not to drown.

## A possible trinity

In a four-sided figure of darkness
you are overcome with joy, humility, service:
such belonging to material.
You are a tenant of the body,
on a licence from the spirit.

Poetry, Malady and Love;
a trinity that the blood consumes,
yet determines to rebirth.

Friday was a favoured day:
so full of my certitude
that nothing could happen outside words.
Their warm stream invades mouth, trachea;

working without end this quadrilateral
of darkness. There, death signs its name
daily in an undisclosed tongue.

## A basket of cherries

With this Sunday's losing lottery-ticket
in the drawer of the afternoon
I try small exercises of levitation.
Everything, now, is the colour of lead
heated to one thousand degrees.
Youth, a stuffed canary
flying towards another fund of words:
no response from the body I inhabit
casually, like a salesman with a sprained ankle.

Weeds have grown on the Marathon Plain.
Now the lighthouse at the Cape of Good Hope
disperses tickets for the Association
of the amateur, voluntary Short-Sighted.

On the screen of my memory, in your place,
there is a beautiful basket of cherries –
still life in the expressionist style,
like some monstrous cell, voracious, bleeding.

On a wooden table, pitted with woodworm,
rolled newspapers are invaded by ants.
In the *Romance* Tristan and Isolde,
such cheap paper. With the sword at p.180
I shred the losing ticket from Sunday.
With a sailboat at p.200, I cross over the sea.


## Eyes that are blind


Your name is forgotten: your smell and taste:
the severe Greek of your body.
Imperial was the curve of your waist.
So who remembers now? Not me.
I'm cured of your forgettable form
as a blind woman ignores night:
or a blind eye sees no harm
in a rocky hazard. You've gone from sight.

# MIRCEA DINESCU

*versions by*

# BRENDAN KENNELLY

MIRCEA DINESCU was born in 1950 in Slobozia, a small provincial town in southern Romania. His first poems were published when he was 17, and he was only 21 when he won the Union of Writers' Debut Prize for his first volume. Further collections appeared in Romania and received further awards from the Writers' Union and the Romanian Academy, but by the late 1980s he and his work were seen as controversial and confrontational, and his final book before the revolution of 1989 could be published only abroad. Because of an interview given to the French newspaper *Libération*, critical of the régime, he was under house arrest from April until the events of 1989. He was active in these days of the revolution and it was he who – with the actor Ion Caramitru – made the first appearance on Romanian television announcing that Ceaucescu had been deposed. Like Blandiana and many other intellectuals and former dissidents, he was part of the Salvation Front in the days before it became a political party. Early in 1990 he was the first freely elected President of the Writers' Union. He is currently the literary director of a newly established and very popular satirical political weekly. His poetry is available in Britain in *Exile on a Peppercorn*, translated by Andrea Deletant and Brenda Walker (Forest Books, 1985).

# The hens

In a castle turned battery
I drank red beetroot wine
with the caretaker and watchman

every night until dawn.
If red turned white in the morning air
we didn't care, we didn't care.

The hens were a bit up in the air
too, turning a blind eye to the carry-on.
They croaked and muffled here and there,

pecking at paintings
scratching at Brueghel the Elder
cackling in the clavichord

plopping eggs in the Biedermayer.
(Savonarola would've fashioned
a handsome cassock from their wattles.)

We were happy and willing
to go lion-hunting
with flypaper

the revolution smelt of baked potato
the loudspeakers drowned all poetry
lamps deepened the darkness

every letter was a strangled cry.
We, too, croaked and muffled.
We, too, turned a blind eye.

## Manuscript found inside a lamp globe

A pair of scissors for cutting fingers
crosses its legs in the letter-box.

On the metropolitan church hill
windows beckon, no shops are visible.

People waiting at the bus stop
accommodate the dwarf walking his abundant hump.

No rationing of death here
but a shortage of fuel, paper, God.

If fools were food, the queue of intellectuals
at the butcher's wouldn't be so long.

## Discovering the works

I thought poetry hid under the heron's wing
or deep in the woods
but like a prophet driven from the desert by oil rigs gurgling

I'm ready to talk it out with reality.

    I was wrong, wrong as can be.

Just now, I'm smashing this wall with a pickaxe.

    See.

# Ridiculous chess

How silly can you be?
Thinking poetry can produce a better world!
As if throwing a lump of sugar
into a tiger's cage
would get it reading Shakespeare.

Toughened by your trouble
(as if you'd been looked after in a mirror)
you whistle like a train at the stations
till you're trampled by the crowd
rushing for that comfortable seat on your nape.

The dream caricatures the real.
Remember
the ridiculous game of chess
the mad bishop moving villages
sacrificing horses
and a thousand people trampling each other
      in haste to praise his game.

## The cows

Take my word for it.
These cows from Holland transported by plane
are the pride of every man and woman

here.
I swear
seven gypsies hired to lull them with music
hide until night among stacks of corn.

Farmhands hiccup in the shower
or sneeze, offended, under the X-ray machine
when the doctor rebukes them for clothes
stinking of tobacco and brandy.

Were it not for the blind villages about us
and the barefoot children disfiguring the fields
these ballerinas would be even heavier with medals.

## Epistle on accepting the reality with a slightly metaphysical postscript

Cool. So cool. Ivy on furnaces.
How can his anger
smash farmlands to pieces?

Quacks at the Ostrich Academy, you quacks full of pride,
we haven't got enough sand
for all the heads we could hide.

So we scribble, scribble on the sly,
Magister Procopius, on the skin of a calf
not yet a twinkle in a bull's eye.

POSTSCRIPT:   We were saddened by the rumour
              that you've taken to heart
              the Pope's infallible hiccups
              while the bells of the Vatican fart.

## Speech against revolt

Barren, hysterical
revolt never brought me fine stretches of land

at night it would slip into my bed
by day, electrocute me in the world outside

give me a melon to live on
and, to lean against, a moving train

because I weaken with hunger when working
my spine a full cartridge belt hanging

bark! bark! I am hunter and hound
even the natives chase through the swampy land

I don't love myself any more, I'll just grow old,
God is a deep-down pocket full of holes,

loneliness goes on manufacturing all kinds
of suicide for humans out of their tiny minds

I want to be born, mother says she's bored,
I want to cry, others' cries are far more gifted,

give me a melon to live on
and, to lean against, a moving train

## Avalanche

The eleventh of November
    at nine in the morning
        I had a date with an eager

avalanche of snow
    on a smoothly seductive slope
        in the Himalayas.

It might have been love at first sight
    but without my passport in hand
        my relatives named in the light

my luggage packed
    my tickets bought
        and myself well sniffed by detectors

the avalanche, at a quarter past nine, in a cool breeze,
    offended, hysterical, ran off down the slope
        with a Greek and two Japanese...

    O God of love at first sight
    please sweeten those institutions of sadness
    that conduct against love and death
    a noble and gutsy fight.

## Factory touching factory


A hundred women run away every month
from the silk factory hostel.

Looms bark empty
the production graph slides towards the floor
the manager's hair turns white
the telephone swears like a trooper
angry green dollars slip back to the West
slogans erupt in flaming letters
meetings reach fever-pitch
trucks bundle girls from encircling villages
        to train, get cop-on and know-how

but a hundred women run away every month

made restless as bulls by the red of the silk
in a bullfight without toreadors or blood.

If the bulldozers came, that'd be good,
to level the ground,
bricklayers, welders,
wolfwhistling drivers,
scruffy tramps, building-site artists,

        let conveyor belts rumble
            let Siemens-Martin furnaces sing
                smell of pitch and coal go on rising

        to calm the girls
            hand in hand
                silk/cast iron

            factory touching factory.

# STEFAN AUGUSTIN DOINAS

*versions by*
## CIARAN CARSON

STEFAN AUGUSTIN DOINAS was born in 1922 in a village near Arad and grad-
uated from the University of Cluj. He made his literary debut in 1944 and
thereafter has published, besides poetry, many works of criticism, essays
and translation. Doinas was a member of the Sibiu Literary Circle, regarded
as a very significant movement in contemporary Romanian literature; the
Circle was established by a group of young Transylvanian intellectuals at
the end of World War II, and then banned after the Communist takeover
a few years later. The first honorary chairman of the Writers' Union and
a member of the Romanian Academy, Doinas is regarded as one of the
doyens of Romanian poetry. Currently he is Editor-in-Chief of *Twentieth
Century*, an international arts review published in Bucharest. Also active in
political life, he sits with the opposition in the Senate, the upper house of
the Romanian parliament. A selection of his work, *Alibi and other poems*,
translated by Peter Jay and Virgil Nemoianu, was published by Anvil Press
in 1975.

## Cortège

I see her on her balcony, the gorgeous fat one, slobbering on
    mandarins
And shivering with laughter, scattering confetti to the March
    winds'

Desultory snowflakes. Meanwhile, down there in The Square,
    three young troubadours
Are cuffed and collared to a rocking tumbrel, drawn not by
    horses

But by out-of-breath philosophers. Wooden drum-wheels hooped
    with argent
Rumble towards the scaffold. Unleavened breadcrumbs lie crushed
    on the pavement.

Like two crawling barbed wire hedges, halberdiers conduct a
    parallel
On either side. Their pikes are glittering with geometry and frost.
    It's cold as hell.

## Siege

The fortress balanced on a lance-tip. Unseen army. The wells
     were clogged,
The smoke kept low. We caught the double-headed eagle and
     we ate its mystagogue.

Epidemics came and went. Familiar atavistic ghosts kept firing
     arrows
From the parapets into the world beyond. Nothing. Only the
     stars

In the wound in the side of the god. Then treason struck at
     midnight and the gate
Capitulated. Cowards kow-towed. Nobody. The dazzling
     pirate

Moon broke out. Still nobody. Afflicted by a strange disease of
     sundered
Gates, we weep eternities of blood. There's nobody. But we,
     we have surrendered.

## Alibi

Remorselessly, in fields and forests, on street corners, on the
    eternal
Altar of the bed, murder is done. Was I there? I stared into the
    terminal

Of my own mirrored pupil, and saw my eye denying it, like one
    hand
Washing clean the other. Where was I then? Everybody wears the
    same Cain brand

Emblazoned on their foreheads. I saw the deed and what it led to.
    Heard the shriek
As well. And then my eyes were decommissioned by the knife.
    But I saw him last week,

And I know he is amongst us. And no, I can't tell his name.
    What name would you
Make up for murderers of their own childhood, who believe lies
    to be true?

The lovers enter the marrowbone of a madman and succumb
    slowly in their pit
Of lime. A croaking black unkindness of ravens has
    cloaked it

In the dark of corpses. All our words were in vain. What flag are
    we supposed
To raise above the citadel? Where should we go? All the roads
    are closed.

O ubiquitous accomplice God, we are accomplices to all
    assassinations.
Gag me, choke me, strangle me, and tell me that there are no
    further destinations.

And finally, it must be left unsaid that those not born to this,
    our vampire family,
Sleep soundly in their beds: they have the final alibi.

## The News

Mouse hopping from mouth to mouth:

For all those child-like souls who crept on all fours through
        loopholes in the city wall;
For deserters from the wars, all drenched in sweat and dust
        beneath their chain-mail;

For the hired assassins crying out for baptism, for those
        historians, provocateurs
Of songs and riddles, who preserve the myth in annotated airs;

For the brief reign of kings who only have an hour to go; for
        mothers-to-be
Who hide their embryos in wombs until they pick their time and
        place to be;

For the epileptics, in whom Lucifer has been condemned to
        genuflect
Forever twitching; for those guided by a star; for that Byzantine
        sect

Whose bishops' ears are stuffed with ceremonial cotton wool,
        who chant of hope
Because they know the true *ennui* of knowing God; for the
        Romish Pope;

For those winged choirs of Pandemonium and Principalities; for
        movie queens
All spellbound by their beauty to the millions gazing at the silent
        screens;

For all those quacks who speculate in pain; for long-dead Draculas
Who re-appear in snap-shot family portraits; for the miraculous

Ontology of life in other galaxies, and all their bat-eared aliens;
And even for myself, the self-deluded author of these simple
        lines:

See me, riding on my spitfire stallion, just back from the
        fairy-story
Where it grazed on live coals: Everyone, please hear The News!
        Believe my story,

The meeting has been cancelled! This, by word of mouth!


## Me and my cousin


'As for the Archaeopteryx – for such I thought it might have
        been – I hopped on to its neck.
It turned out to be an alabaster blue. Its name was really Roc.

Syllables of evening stars becoming Lucifers dropped from its
        beak;
Three deep infernos, funnel-grey, were born within its awful look.

Over and above the stratosphere I flew; from noon to dewy eve
        I whirled,
Till I glanced down and noticed it had laid an egg. The egg was
        called The World.'

'Yes,' my cousin said, 'mind you, this Dodo – Roc or
        Archaeopteryx – does not exist.'
'No, it don't,' I answered, as I grappled with its neck, 'I know it
        don't exist.'

# The poet as snow-merchant


When spring has sprung and disappeared the snow, and
    youngsters want to laugh at grown-
Ups, but find – instead of snowdrifts – brothers, parents
    (ready-made folk), then the clown

Appears, this crazy who sells snow. Hibernian winter permafrosts
    his soul;
He haggles like a madman with his naked trees, his frozen birds
    and ice-floes

Creaking like somnivolent Antarctica. He speaks of seeds as
    unexploded
Atom bombs. Swans drift by in caravanserai across the
    colour-coded

Blue ice of one eye; you could catch a pike in the pupil-black
    bullet-hole
Drilled in the other. He hawks his merchandise remorselessly,
    and being snow

Himself, he spreads himself about: a scattered aftermath of
    downy pillow-
Feathers marks the progress of his unseen army, in which all
    the jolly fellows

Carry brooms instead of ostrich plumes; the mayor's statue they
    denounce as being hollow.

## Bird

No. How should I know what you call that fowl you crane your
        neck towards as it
Passes overhead? I've never come across it.

For all I know, it has the squawk-box of a coot, the awkward
        stagger
Of a stork. Could it be a Stuka?

Fucked if I know. What dreck does it eat? Does it spend life on
        the wing?
Does it regurgitate? Or sing?

Are the Easter eggs it lays in monasteries egg-shaped? Does it
        wear
Frankincense or myrrh? Or swear?

All I know is this refrain: hello, hello, you nightmare archipelago,
I don't know birdshit from guano.

CIARAN CARSON

# The words

Yes – someone lived here once. You know it by the pungent
    dragon-whiff,
The way a zephyr blows a ghostly music from those conches,
    like the hieroglyph

Of where we are. The dog-rough breath that slabbered here is
    now a mere miasma,
Baffled that the structure of the universe should be corpuscled
    in its plasma.

Hear? The deep vast stratum of a limestone sea still broadcasts
    sound-waves, and
The guardian angels of its threshold are connected to us by an
    ampersand

When we talk in our sleep. There have been other revenants,
    of course: whole asylums
Of escaped lunatics, diatribes of Vandals reared on horse-shit,
    Crusaders and credendums.

Here, consonants have been eclipsed, and vowels carry umlauts,
    like the moan
Of lovers who repaired here to strip off their shadows before
    swoon-
Ing into one another's arms. Now, it is a reservoir of silence,
    or a Twilight Zone...

## Snap

I love it when the photograph becomes a tiger with its yawning
    jaws
About to snaffle up a chunk of time. And we put on a pose,
    because

We are alive and smiling in its eyes, luminous beneath the April
    blue.
We forget the bloodied mill-race underneath; we're already
    swallowed in its whirlpool.

## A pair

All human kind deserves love. But the lunatic who tries to plait
    a rope
Of sand in order to lassoo the newly-risen moon, and by this
    trope

Be levitated; the other dope who, stooped over a river of gold,
    spends all
His life in moulding it to the shape of the faceless wind, to
    give us all

A newly-minted coinage: this odd pair can hitch themselves
    to my star
Any time. And when I'm not at home, you'll know for sure
    they are.

# ILEANA MĂLĂNCIOIU

*versions by*
## MICHAEL LONGLEY

ILEANA MĂLĂNCIOIU was born in 1940 in the Arges region. She studied
philosophy through to doctorate level at the University of Bucharest. Her
first volume of poetry was published in 1967. For many years she was one
of the chief editors of the leading literary magazine *Romanian Life*, and she
has also worked for Romanian television. Her work is influenced greatly
by folklore, and by religious imagery drawn particularly from the Old
Testament. During the early 1980s her collection *Climbing the Mountain*
became celebrated as a challenge to the régime; despite its themes of protest
and its identification of the misery of contemporary Romanian life, it some-
how slipped through the net of censorship, with dire consequences for the
publisher.

## Naive and sentimental painting

We are sitting on two chairs face to face
I have absolutely nothing more to say to you, it's over
I look around as I would at the wall behind a pulpit
Where a gaudy mural of the devil catches the eye.

I laugh at his tail growing longer before my eyes
I laugh at the cauldron of pitch, I laugh at everything
I would laugh at the devoutness of my search for you
But I can't quite manage that yet.

I wouldn't change much in this naive and sentimental
Painting of a hell in which you appear to me
But I would like to tinker with the devil himself
I would like to doodle moustaches on his face.

I would like to rip him off the wall
Taking wall and all if that is all I am up to
I would like to set you free from that chair
Where you gawk devotedly at him.

## Somewhere in Transylvania

Somewhere in Transylvania in an old church
I saw a saint who carried his skin on his back
But the skin had kept the shape of his body
Just as the saint had held on to his faith.

You could see this from his radiant forehead
And from the raw ribs that didn't seem to hurt
And from the way the skin, his facsimile,
Didn't look in the least light-weight.

Somewhere in Transylvania in an old church
I saw a single body that was prepared to die
He carried his soul on his back in his own skin
As though he was carrying a fortune.


## Prayer

King Oedipus was led by the hand by his daughter Antigone
King Lear by Cordelia, the daughter he banished
From his kingdom for, he alleged, not loving him enough
As for you, I could lead you, father, any time

As for me, I've no idea if there will be anyone
To chaperon me at that cataclysmic moment
When the whole show is blacked out from my eyes
I realise this won't be feasible for everyone.

Dear God, don't blind us all at the same time
Take only every second soul and put off for a while
The last act of the tragedy, and let everybody
Have somebody to lead him gently by the hand.

## The beginning of the end

Dead silence. The beginning of the end
A deep grave is being dug very slowly
Now and then the earth caves in on someone
Who dies a suffocating death.

All his relatives scrape with their nails
For the body of the loved one buried alive
Without giving death a thought
They dig slowly into the grey earth.

He had been digging, the story will go
Digging a long time at the grave
And just then the earth caved in
Over those hunched shoulders of his.

No one was near, the others were digging
As well but somewhere else
                              a deep grave
Is being dug very slowly, and now and then
The earth caves in on someone.

## Nightmare

The town filled up with dead people
Who had swarmed on to the main street
Dressed in their Sunday best, clothes
Not to be seen dead in normally.

They stampeded past us laughing
They hadn't a clue what was going on
There were so many they left no room
For those of us still alive and kicking.

We were scared stiff by this mass hysteria
But we stood and gawked as at a carnival
For each of us knew someone in the crowd
And didn't want them locked in the graveyard.

## Samson's hair

Delilah had done her job
Samson's head lay in her lap
As on a tray
His hair cut off and his strength
Lost without his knowing it.

When he woke up and tried to untie
The ropes that bound him, it was too late
But the story can have no ending
While Samson is alive.

Everyone knows how he lost his strength
I remember what happens next
And I stand petrified in the huge hall
Near the two gilded pillars
And wait for Samson's hair to grow.

# Pianoforte

The portrait above the piano
Had got into the black shiny wood
But the pianist wasn't aware that
He was jabbing his fingers into its eyes
While everyone sat transfixed.

I myself had forgotten about everything
But while I took off on a musical high
Above the orchestra, I noticed
How the portrait reproduced in the piano
Hung quite motionless

Like the sword of Damocles
Over the bloke at the keyboard
And could have seen fine well
How he was jabbing his fingers into its eyes
Just to keep me happy.

A good thing he didn't know
He had got into the black shiny wood
And how in that ever so somber concert hall
I all of a sudden pictured him
Sticking his tongue out at the pianist.

# I can't complain

I can't complain of hunger
My food comes free out of the sky
But I worry about the god
Who will have to tuck-in to me.

I'm so gloomy, so depressed
As food for a god I might taste
Even stringier than I am
An even bitterer mouthful.

In a field full of pretty poppies
He might well spit my blood out
And set my fleshy bits aside
To be disposed of among the poor.


# In my brain

In my brain stood the mountain I had been looking up to
Upended, diminished, interred
So there'd be room to take it with me
The day I left.

What's in your brain, they asked me
A mountain, I replied imperturbably
And they grabbed me and hustled me off mountain and all
With me leaning nonchalantly against the sunny cliffs.

They extracted the whole mountain stone by stone
And gazed for a while into my freshly shaved skull
As into a translucent egg
And it seemed even more impenetrable to them.

## The Tower of Babel

We had devised a new method of communicating
Despite the scrambling of all our lingos
We had finished building the Tower of Babel
Which was tall and nicely situated

I don't know when it started to teeter or when
Your man thought it was high time to climb
Up to us and scramble our lingos again
But there was nothing left for him to scramble

For we all spoke the same lingo
I mean, we all said exactly the same thing
And he watched in silence as we bawled out the same word
Which meant absolutely nothing at all.

# MARIN SORESCU

*versions by*
# PAUL MULDOON

MARIN SORESCU was born in a peasant village in Oltenia in 1936, and went on to study philosophy and philology at the University of Iasi. With an international reputation as both poet and playwright, he is perhaps the most translated and best known abroad of contemporary Romanian writers. He has worked as the editor of various literary magazines and currently is Editor-in-Chief of *Literatorul.* Sorescu was enormously popular during the worst years of the repressive Ceaucescu régime in the 1980s when his work was sold in editions of hundreds of thousands. In 1994-95 he was Minister of Culture. He has published two books of poetry with Bloodaxe in Britain, *Selected Poems* (1983) and *The Biggest Egg in the World* (1987); a new selection, *Censored Poems*, is due in 1997.

## Shakespeare

Shakespeare created the world in seven days.

On the first day he made the sky, the mountains, the narrow
      defiles of the soul.
On the second he made the rivers, the seas, the oceans
and sundry other emotions
which he doled out to Hamlet, Julius Caesar, Antony and Cleopatra,
      Ophelia,
Othello and such,
emotions which would preside over them and their descendants
for ever and ever.
On the third day he assembled all the people
and gave them their tastes:
a taste of happiness, of love, of despondency,
of jealousy, a taste of glory and so on
until there were no tastes left.

As for the poor fellows who got there too late,
he gave them each a pat on the head
and told them there was nothing left for them
but to become literary critics
and quibble over his work.
The fourth and fifth days were reserved for laughter.
He sent in the clowns
to do somersaults
and he even allowed kings, emperors
and other unfortunates a little comic relief.
On the sixth day he solved some administrative problems:
he wrote in a tempest
and taught King Lear
how to wear a crown of straw.
With the odds and ends left over from making the world
he created Richard III.
On the seventh day he looked around to see what was still to be done.
The theatre directors had already covered the world with posters
so Shakespeare reckoned that after so much work
he deserved to take in a show
but he now felt so completely exhausted
that he went to die for a bit.

## Destiny

The hen I bought last night,
the frozen hen,
had come to life again
and, after laying the biggest egg in the world,
was awarded the Nobel Prize.

This phenomenal egg
was passed from hand to hand
and went around the world in a matter of weeks
and around the sun
in three hundred and sixty-five days.

The hen was given buckets of money
that had been converted to buckets of grain,
though she simply wasn't able to eat it all

because she was invited here, there and everywhere
to address conferences, give personal interviews,
and have her photograph taken.

The reporters often made a point
of having me pose
beside her.
And so, after having dedicated
my life to art,
I suddenly became famous
as a poultry-breeder.

## Chess

I move a white day,
he moves a black.
I venture a dream,
he takes it.
He attacks my lungs,
I think about it all year in hospital.
I make a brilliant combination
and win only a black day.
He moves a misfortune
and threatens me with cancer
(just now it takes the shape of a cross)
but I put a book in front of him
and force him to retreat.
I win a few more pieces here and there
but, let's face it, half my life
is strewn by the side of the board.
'I put you in check and you'll not be so optimistic,'
he tells me.
'Never mind,' I reply,
'I'll castle my feelings.'

Over my shoulder, my wife and children
and the sun and the moon and the other hangers-on
are biting their nails with every move I make.

I light another cigarette
and keep on playing.

## Symmetry

There I was, out taking a stroll,
when suddenly, ahead of me,
two roads opened up –
one to the right,
the other to the left,
in keeping with the rules of symmetry.

I stood there,
screwed up my eyes,
pursed my lips
and, after clearing my throat,
took the one to the right
(exactly the one I shouldn't have taken,
as it turned out).

Things pottered along as they tend to potter along –
I won't bother you with the details –
until there opened up ahead of me
two chasms,
one to the right
and another to the left.

I threw myself into the left one
without batting an eyelid, without a moment's thought,
and I plunged down into that left chasm
which was not, alas, lined with feathers.
I dragged myself on
and on and on
when suddenly, ahead of me,
two roads opened up expansively.
'I'll show you this time,' I said to myself
and, out of spite, took the one to the left.
Wrong again, terribly wrong. The one to the right
was the true, true road – the great road, as they say.
At the very first crossroads
I gave myself over entirely
to the road on my right. Same again.
I should have taken the other one. The other one...

My food has almost gone now
and my walking-stick's so gnarled
it no longer brings forth buds
in whose shade I might rest
when I'm in despair.

Not only are my bones ground down by stones
but they moan and groan
about how I've consistently failed them.

And now, there open up ahead of me
two heavens,
one to the right,
the other to the left.

## Ceramic

The archaeologists have unearthed
somewhere in the archaeological dig of my body
a clay pot.

It's in the shape of a heart.
On it an anonymous craftsman
from long before the Christian era
painted a few rays of the sun.

Others have come along
and added their five cents' worth,
interspersing the rays with various folk motifs.

I, too, have made my mark on the pot
with the scratches and scrapings of a new epoch,
so that the researchers of the year four thousand
will be able to date me
to the middle of the twentieth century,
roughly speaking.

## Angle

The cranes flying by, with their rigid form,
might be sonnets for peasants on their farm.

## Persecution mania

You tax me
and I believe you
tax me.

You send my child
to war
and I somehow believe you
send my child
to war.

You take away my days
yet I believe you
take away
my days.

## Precaution

Be sure to check on your sleeping position.
Before you settle down to dream
take a lantern in your hand
and notice that neither your thoughts
nor the fingers of your hand stray,
see that they both stay.

If your knees are up to your mouth
and your breath is as hot as an ox's at the manger,
it's hard for the Saviour to slip through.
That's not a good position for you.

If you favour one side over the other,
all the sand will trickle
out of your ear into a great sandbank.
There are many deserts,
I can say without a shadow of a doubt,
into which everyone has simply run down and out.

If you lie facing the ceiling,
try at least to make the soles of your feet reach
to the edge of the sky,
or a few centimetres over the edge of the sky,
in case you do arise on the third day
and could use a little leverage to help you on your way.

As I say, mind how you go to sleep.
The mountains themselves tend to be out of kilter,
always seeming to be askew
from your soul's somewhat limited point of view.

## Solemnly

I would carry
the full of my arms of papers
into a big field,
solemnly signing them and solemnly
plowing them under
with the swing-plow.

To see what might come
of these thoughts,
from joys, from happiness and unhappiness,
through winter, spring, summer and autumn.

Now I'm stepping
the black field,
hands behind my back,
more anxious with every passing day.

Surely it can't be the case
that not one of my letters was good?

Surely the day will come
when this field will be a field full of flames
and I will pass among them, solemnly,
wearing a crown like Nero?

## Fresco

In Hell the sinners
are used to maximum effect.

Women have hair-clips, pins, rings and bracelets
taken off their heads
with tongs and tweezers.
Their linen and nighties are also removed.
Then they're thrown
into seething cauldrons
to make sure the pitch doesn't boil over.

Others are rendered down
for the lunch-pails
full of warmed-over sins
that are left on the doorsteps of devil-pensioners.

Men tend to be used
for the hardest work,
except for the very hairy ones,
who are woven again
into carpets and doormats.

## Or something like that

I took the last plane out (there was standing room for one only –
much cheaper, of course),
and I could see down below people scurrying about
like iron filings.
'It's a contest for pedestrians,' I was told,
'having to do with the zebra crossing. Whoever gets there first
doesn't have to wait. There's nothing to wait for.'

When the plane reached cruising altitude, as high
as it was allowed to fly that day,
I suddenly got very scared,
standing there, looking at the clouds.
'Stop,' I cried, 'Stop. I want to get off.
I'm seasick. I hope you don't mind
if I'm seasick in an airplane.'

And, as it happens, the plane stopped. The emergency door
opened
and I got off.
Everything was so topsy-turvy that I didn't land on the earth
(it would have been difficult from that height, in any case,
since I had no parachute-training).
I landed on the moon. And the moon
was in her ninth month. A big, full moon.

And the moon gave birth to me as soon as I started to struggle,
wailing, whimpering, wanting to get off
obsessively now. The moon gave birth to me
and it was, by all accounts, an easy delivery.
Was this the second or third time? What odds, as Lazarus would say.
The moon or some other planet? Who gives a hoot?

But I don't always recognise myself any more.
I keep pinching and pawing myself. I consult little, old crones,
the zodiac, the heavenly charts.
I don't recognise myself up close.
And, inside me, someone still whimpers and whines
though their whines are muffled by their swaddling-clothes,

'Stop. Stop. I want to get off.'

## O, Gods

In the middle of the night,
in the heart of the city,
the wood of the wooden horse of Troy creaks weirdly
and the Trojans quite anxiously
ask themselves:

What further calamity
lies in store?
It's a bad omen, is it not,
when the wooden horse creaks
for no apparent reason,
like an old bomb left over from the last war,
in the very heart of the city?

O, Gods.

## Superstition

My cat is washing herself
with her left paw.
There's going to be a war.

I've noticed, you must understand,
that every time she washes herself
with her left paw,
international tension mounts
considerably.

How is it she can have a grasp
of all five continents?
Could it be that Pythia has swum
into her pupils,
the one who could foresee
the whole of history
without the benefit of punctuation?

I could cry out loud
to think that not only I myself
but the sky-load of souls I've tied
to my back
should depend at the end of the day
on the whim of a pussy-cat.

So go and catch a mouse or two
rather than fomenting
global warfare,
you hag,
you hellcat, you ham-fisted hoor.

# MIHAI URSACHI

## *versions by*
## PAULA MEEHAN

MIHAI URSACHI was born in 1941 in Romanian Moldavia and graduated from the University of Iasi in philosophy and German studies. He has chosen never to be a part of what he has called 'the poetic business' of the capital, Bucharest. Despite having published only intermittently since his first volume in 1970, he has maintained his substantial reputation and popularity within Romania. He was imprisoned for four years during the 1960s after conviction on a political charge. In 1981 he was able to emigrate to the United States where he lived for nine years before returning after the revolution to run the National Theatre in Iasi. He is now active in the opposition Civic Alliance.

# Imperium

## I *Invocation*

Today my soul approaches Your Holy of Holies.
I stand before You without the agony
without the ecstasy of those enslaved
by delusion. I come to Your threshold
with limitless knowledge of the limited.

Your golden voice cast a spell
over my waking nights. I shed
the blood of my beloved in Your name.
In a fever I devoured life
like some savage creature of the woods.

Your voice was the thundering tale.
And I pledged myself to Your service.
In that moment's glimpse was the endless
forced marches in the desert, the endless
troubles of my army.

Now, like a pillar of glass in the wasteland,
my soul stands untroubled before Your tidalwave of gold.
I offer what you cannot know, O All Knowing.
Receive this my viaticum.
My gift of fire and ice

I surrender to Your blinding glory.

## II

My empire was the desert. My deeds
were witnessed by great pyramids, overseers
to my unfolding destiny. There were voices dirgeful,
the lilies of the field wasting their sweetness
in holy chant, numbering my failures,
uttering sacred verses, celebrating my deeds.
All that glory rang out like a psalm
in the lonely reaches of the Sphinx.

But to get to the heart of the matter:
I want to speak of the lust for virgin biood;
of the spear violating the blossom;
of the head of my beloved falling to my feet.
This was the price. This was the price of empire.
I paid this price for my desert.
I made a chalice of my beloved's skull.
Drink from it all you who are not yet born.

My deeds, my great ambitions heralded
by choirs of angels: let me inscribe them for you.
I'll tell you a story. I'll leave nothing out.
Not the betrayals, the treachery, the gory details
of poisonings, of stranglings, of the knife in the back.
It's all written down already, embossed in gold
on the heavy purple of empire: Signs
made purposely with no way to decode them.

### III

My love, don't be charmed by that voice you hear.
It is a ghost whispering a tale to enchant you,
a vampire hungry for virgin blood.
Let us walk together on this clear shore,
let us walk with peace in our hearts,
calmly under the moon's protection.
Have faith, my love. Come with me now
to the hill, we'll climb to the Scythian tomb.

Under this ghostly light the ocean is a pale army
of marching spectres, they sing in their chains
to the stars; the constellations are huge galleys
driven by slaves of the deep wheeling above us.
Under the moon's protection, The Great Lily
has been awaiting us for two thousand years.

All that exists, exists. All that exists, exists forever.
Death has no dominion. Apparition, vision,
is the true history of the tides of blood, the red nightmare,
all that the empire cost, the sojourn in the desert.
Do not listen, my love, to the ghost's ravings.
There is only ourselves. Come to the hill in Luxor,
in Egypt. We'll climb to our destiny.

IV *The True and Complete History of Sagittarius*

Once on an island in a lake in a forest
we gathered together, a clear starry night.
We carried light armour, in motley we dressed,
the moon cast over us her windfall of light.

And then loud cries broke the stillness,
we formed in ranks, we whirled, we froze.
Out of the forest's primal darkness
we conjured a vision, as one we rose

to behold the glory of a bison's head.
*It cut right through me with its cold
fixed stare.* Between its horns mounted:
a water-lily wrought of shining gold.

Each one of us was destined to enter
the magic circle, there present our voivodal symbol,
wreathed and bearing the bow of an archer
with a single shaft, an arrow of crystal.

I knelt in the circle burdened down with the weight
of my emblems, my duty. I loosed my arrow
at the heart of the water-lily – over the sea of fate,
the island, the starry night, the fallen snow.


V

*Rightly or wrongly? Justice or injustice? Consider:*
First he was given to the executioner who chopped off both his hands.
They were like two fish beached on a mound of hands.
*That's what they do to prisoners. That's what they do to their hands.*
After a month they cut off his arms to the elbows.
*That's what they do to thieves. That's what they do to their arms.*
Then they ripped out his tongue. *Perjury! Perjury!*
They poked out his eyes with a red-hot spike.
*That is the fate of those who bear false witness.*
With the string of a melodious bow they garrotted him in the dark.
*Oh that is the fate of all who are born. The fate of the born.*

## VI *The Game*

My lady, let's play a little game,
I'll be Attila. Ildiko be your name.
Taken by force, my captive bride
In my tent of furs let us hide.

It's only a game. I give you a toast:
*Once upon a time there was an Emperor...*
Like the mad we see ghosts,
The wedding guests flock to the mirror.

Lord, can you tell me why the river runs red?
And Lord, can you tell me it's name?
My Lady, I can't tell why the river runs red
But I know the Danube is its name.

Lord, do my brothers sleep in the arms
Of the river's red rolling water?
And does my father drown in its arms?
Won't you answer his only daughter?

My Lord, these things lie deep in the past,
I'll tell you my dream, my vision.
Come close. The lock of the door is fast.
This is my only passion.

In my dream we were children long ago
Away in the far green Septentrion.
Our nurse is reading a tale of woe
From the Book of Marcel Brion.

I'll teach you what strange game we played
Back then, with daggers, and flames, and blood.
Lord, I will teach you what game we played
If you'll lend me your dagger, your hood.

This game will go down in the history books –
The most beautiful game ever played.
*...on the steppe, dust was thick over stooks,*
*the cranes long wail and the day's slow fade.*

**VII** *The Author's Confession: his shortcomings in the face
of the world, the passage of time, and this, his Imperium.*

Here is the author; He comes bearing a lily on his shoulder as if it
        were a carbine.
Armed in such a fashion, everything that exists in the world
        wounds him.
Often he says:
'Oh wound:
your name is Art.'
Given that he cuts so ridiculous a figure, all he turns his hand to
        is in vain,
just like the mason, his brother,
who wanted to erect a pyramid in Ticău.
Not to mention the fact that time's running out
the hour is getting late and his tools are, to put it bluntly, modest.
Much as it grieves him, he forwards you the following story:

VIII *The Old Chronologists*

Two old fellows had been cell mates a long long time, in that dungeon from which there is no exit. They could not say exactly how long they had been there, although they counted meticulously each day as it passed; and with the help of the monk Damaschin's digital calendar, they kept track on their knuckles of Holy Days and other important dates over a cycle of many thousands of years. You might call them expert chronologists, since they could tell at the drop of a hat on what date precisely the Easter of 1054 fell, in the year the two churches separated. Or whether that day in 1453 had been a Thursday or a Friday, in the year Constantinople was taken by the Turks. One might suddenly utter: The 24th of April in the year 11,007 will be the Tuesday before Palm Sunday...

Their ambition was a complete chronology of the entire cycle of sixteen thousand years.

There was no telling how long they had been in that cell, though they could remember the exact day of their arrival and the exact number of days that had passed since.

After a long time they said: the complete cycle for sixteen thousand years is recorded on the knucklebones of our fingers and we know for certain that sixteen thousand years from today it will be the Tuesday before Palm Sunday.

Then one of them let out a long sigh and said: Listen. I am going to die. I leave the chronology in your custody.

And the other one said: I'm not feeling too good myself.

Then, looking at their mummified knuckles, with the skin like parchment, on which were minutely marked the sixteen thousand years, they both dropped dead.

It was the Tuesday. Before Palm Sunday.

## IX

Here, we have peace beyond understanding. We surely have peace.

The wild plum tree has cast its blossoms to your feet,
an angel has sown the whole hillside with flowers,
The ones we call *Immortelle*. Every year
a red field poppy blooms in my heart. Night has fallen
and the wild plum tree has cast down its blossoms.
The fathomless sea guards the white silences
and all our speech has drowned. The moon
like something out of an old sacred poem
spins her light over the lily-shaped stones. The lily
thinks: this is what we were when we passed along the shore
of the fathomless sea. The whole universe become a lily.

Here, we have peace beyond understanding. We surely have peace.


## X *Postscript: What the acolyte scratched on the white limestone of the Scythian Tomb*

My love, you who don't exist
with your sad dark eyes
from the place where you don't exist
watching me with your sad dark eyes,

from behind the silver wall
that separates all things,
the phantom from the real,
the mortal from immortal beings,

from the depths of your time,
so close and out of reach
with your sad dark eyes,
my lily-faced love, you watch.


— CARMEN EXPLICIT —